SPOTLIGHT
ON CHILDREN'S
AUTHORS

BRIAN SELZNICK

JOSEPH KAMPFF

Cavendish
Square
New York

Published in 2014 by Cavendish Square Publishing, LLC
303 Park Avenue South, Suite 1247, New York, NY 10010
Copyright © 2014 by Cavendish Square Publishing, LLC
First Edition

This publication represents the opinions and views of the author based on his or her personal experience, knowledge, and research. The information in this book serves as a general guide only. The author and publisher have used their best efforts in preparing this book and disclaim liability rising directly or indirectly from the use and application of this book.

CPSIA Compliance Information: Batch #WW14CSQ

All websites were available and accurate when this book was sent to press.

Library of Congress Cataloging-in-Publication Data
Kampff, Joseph.
Brian Selznick / Joseph Kampff.
pages cm — (Spotlight on children's authors)
Includes bibliographical references.
ISBN 978-1-62712-265-8 (hardcover) ISBN 978-1-62712-266-5 (paperback) ISBN 978-1-62712-267-2 (ebook)
1. Selznick, Brian. 2. Illustrators—United States—Biography. I. Title.

NC975.5.S43K36 2014
741.6'42092—dc23
[B]

2013030824

Editorial Director: Dean Miller
Senior Editor: Peter Mavrikis
Copy Editor: Cynthia Roby
Art Director: Jeffrey Talbot
Designer: Amy Greenan
Production Manager: Jennifer Ryder-Talbot
Production Editor: Andrew Coddington
Photo research by Julie Alissi, J8 Media

The photographs in this book are used by permission and through the courtesy of: Cover photo by Gareth Cattermole/Staff/Getty Images Entertainment/Getty Images; Michael Buckner/Staff/Getty Images Entertainment/Getty Images, 4; © AP Images, 6; © Jan Nagle, 8, 14, 19, 21, 30; Popperfoto/Contributor/Popperfoto/Getty Images, 16; Joseph Scherschel/Contributor/Time & Life Pictures/Getty Images, 17; Joseph Scherschel/Time & Life Pictures/Getty Images, 18–19; David Corio/Contributor/Michael Ochs Archives/Getty Images, 22; © Photos 12 / Alamy, 24; © Paramount Pictures/ZUMA Press, 27; Michael Loccisano/Staff/Getty Images Entertainment/Getty Images, 28; Stephen Chernin/Stringer/Getty Images News/Getty Images, 33; Splash News/Newscom, 34.

Printed in the United States of America

CONTENTS

INTRODUCTION: A Few Important

Things to Know About Brian Selznick

Brian Selznick loves automata, dinosaurs, and old movies. His apartment is full of odds and ends—mostly odds—like parts from old watches he bought in France and a rather large collection of snow globes. He's kind of a tall guy and he wears glasses. His glasses are round, like Harry Potter's. He's a wonderful public speaker, and he's extremely nice. And Brian Selznick likes to draw—a lot.

Brian is the author and illustrator of *The Invention of Hugo Cabret*, a massive and wildly imaginative picture book that is itself filled with all kinds of odds and ends, such as clockwork and automata (a fancy word for robots). A famous filmmaker named Martin Scorsese made the book into a movie call *Hugo*. Brian is amazed that this happened. Brian has written and illustrated other picture books too, including *The Houdini Box* and, most recently, *Wonderstruck*. He's also illustrated a bunch of books for other writers. And he's a puppeteer.

Brian's creativity and imagination shines through in his illustrations.

Chapter 1
A CHILDREN'S BOOK ILLUSTRATOR WHO ALMOST WASN'T

Brian Selznick was born on July 14, 1966, in East Brunswick, New Jersey. He's the oldest of three children. Brian's parents, Lynn and Roger Selznick, worked hard to help their kids achieve their goals. Brian's dad had always wanted to be an archaeologist, but his mom pressured him into becoming an accountant instead. He wasn't able to do the job he really wanted, and he wasn't going to let his kids make the same mistake. Brian explains, "One of the things my dad always said was he wanted us kids to do what we wanted to do. When I was little, I wanted to be an artist, my sister wanted to be a kindergarten teacher, and my brother wanted to be a brain surgeon—and that's what we've all grown up to be." Thinking back on his childhood, Brian says, "I grew up drawing, reading books, and watching movies. I eventually grew up and became a writer and illustrator of children's books, a job that combines all my childhood loves."

Ever since he was little, Brian made things with his hands. "I remember when I was a kid one of the first things I had ever made was a tinfoil sculpture of dinosaurs," Brian says. "The story in my

Remy Charlip was a
favorite of Selznick
growing up.

family is that when I was around three or four I would go to my grandmother's house and her maid would give me tinfoil to keep me out of trouble, and that's when I started making...dinosaur tinfoil sculptures." Brian loved to build things, and when he was a kid he built an "Island of G.I. Joe" in his backyard to play in and a house for his troll dolls. When the Selznicks' dog chewed the arm off one of his trolls, Brian used clay to make a new arm for it. He even mixed colors to perfectly match the troll's skin color.

Creativity runs in Brian's family. He's distantly related to David O. Selznick, an important early Hollywood film producer who made movies from the 1920s to the 1950s. Many of David's movies, such as the original *King Kong* and *Gone with the Wind*, are still famous today. Brian loved to watch old movies, and *King Kong* was one of his favorites when he was a kid. He especially liked the scene in which King Kong fights a tyrannosaurus rex and a triceratops. He also loved science fiction movies such as *Star Wars*. He still has drawings of Darth Vader and Princess Leia that he made when he was ten years old.

Brian's favorite picture book when he was a kid was *Fortunately* by Remy Charlip. He loved the way the story came together with each turn of the page. "We watch what happens as Ned, page by page, tries to get from New York to a surprise party in Florida," Brian recalls. "Having fortunately borrowed a friend's airplane, which has unfortunately exploded, he fortunately finds himself with a parachute that unfortunately has a hole in it, and so on. The story moves forward after each line of text, always bringing a surprise when we turn the pages." Brian still thinks the book is hilarious.

Brian started drawing when he was very young. "Even in kindergarten I remember drawing and having the other kids gather around because they liked what I was drawing," Brian says. "I recently found my kindergarten report card and it says, 'Brian is a good artist.' So I guess I've always been drawing." The public school Brian attended in East Brunswick had great art programs. "My teachers knew that I loved to draw but I hated going to gym class," Brian remembers. "Sometimes they would allow me to go to art class instead of gym, which always felt like a victory!" Even though the school encouraged his creativity, Brian's love of drawing sometimes got him into trouble. "I know sometimes I got in trouble in school for drawing monsters," Brian explains. "But I really loved drawing monsters, so I kept at it, and then eventually I made a book about a kid who loved monsters." In addition to the art classes he took at school, Brian's parents let him take private lessons after school to help him develop his talent.

Although Brian knew he wanted to have a job that involved art, he didn't want to be a children's book illustrator at first. "I think because everybody told me in high school that I should illustrate children's books, it made me really, really not want to do that," he says. "I sort of rebelled against it." After high school, Brian went to an art school called the Rhode Island School of Design (RISD, pronounced *Riz-dee*). "I thought I was going to be a set designer for the theater. Because I used to love to act in shows and I used to love to build and design the sets for the different shows. So I took some classes to learn about theater, and then I took a lot of classes just to practice drawing." He also studied theater at Brown University, which is not far from RISD.

Brian's rebellion against illustrating may have gone too far sometimes, and he missed some major opportunities to learn a lot about children's books. "At RISD there are some very famous illustrators that teach there like, Chris Van Allsburg and David MacAulay, but since I didn't want to be a children's book illustrator when I was in school I never took any classes with them," he explains. And when Maurice Sendak—the person who created *Where the Wild Things Are*—made a special appearance at RISD, Brian refused to go hear him speak. "Everyone was clamoring to get in," Brian says. "Now I feel extremely stupid."

Students enjoying the RISD campus in Providence, Rhode Island

Brian graduated from RISD in 1988. He applied to the Yale School of Drama to study set design, but he wasn't accepted into the program. "So I traveled for a little while, and I came back, and I realized that the things I love most are telling stories," Brian says. "I love drawing, and I've always loved kids, and that's when I realized that in fact maybe I should be illustrating children's books." Brian knew exactly what he wanted to do, but there was just one catch. He didn't know how to do it. "So when I finished college and decided that I did not want to be a set designer and that I wanted to be an illustrator for kids' books, I had a little problem," he explains. "I had not studied children's book illustration in school."

The first book Brian published was a picture book called *The Houdini Box*.

Chapter 2
ILLUSTRIOUS ILLUSTRATOR EXTRAORDINAIRE!

Not only had Brian not studied children's book illustration in school, he hadn't even read many children's books when he was a kid. "I never really liked reading as a kid. I had a couple of books that I loved, but I spent a lot of time seeing the movies of the books that I should have read," Brian says. In 1989, Brian got a job at Eeyore's Books for Children in New York City. "I kind of charmed my way into the job because you were supposed to have an extensive knowledge of children's literature to get the job, and I certainly did not," explains Brian. In addition to selling kids' books, Brian painted the store windows for holidays and special events: "The first was Anthony Browne. He was going to read from his book, *Gorilla*. So I painted this giant nine-foot gorilla directly on the glass."

Brian learned all about kids' books at Eeyore's. "I got my real education in children's books from my boss Steve Geck who sent me home every night with bags of his favorite books," Brian says. "I discovered books I'd never seen before and became reacquainted with ones I loved, like *Fortunately*, or books I'd forgotten, like *Where the Wild Things Are.*" Brian's boss seemed to know everything about children's books. He could even guess which new books were going to win major awards, like the Caldecott Medal. "His accuracy always amazed me," Brian says. When the Caldecott Medal winners were announced, the store would get rolls of gold stickers to put on the winning books. "I distinctly remember putting the stickers on *Officer Buckle and Gloria* by Peggy Rathmann. I loved the feel of those stickers, their thickness and shine," Brian says. Brian liked the stickers so much that he stole some of them when he stopped working at Eeyore's. "I figured this would be the closest I would ever come to those pretty gold seals," he admits.

Brian's education at Eeyore's paid off in 1991 when he published his first picture book, *The Houdini Box.* Brian was still working at Eeyore's when he created the book. In fact, his boss and his boss's girlfriend helped Brian get the book published. *The Houdini Box* is about a boy named Victor who idolizes the famous magician Harry Houdini. Victor practices his own magic act at home, escaping from locked closets and holding his breath underwater in the bathtub. At first, Victor doesn't believe he'll ever be as great as Houdini, but soon after he meets Houdini, Victor receives a mysterious box that may contain the secrets to Houdini's magic.

Houdini was a real magician and escape artist who lived from 1874 to 1926. He was one of Brian's heroes when Brian was a kid. "I loved that he could escape from anything in the world and I loved how mysterious he was," he says. Storytelling is a kind of magic for Brian. He loves stories because they allow readers to meet people

WHAT IS THE CALDECOTT MEDAL?

The Caldecott Medal is an award given to "the artist of the most distinguished American Picture Book for Children published in the United States during the preceding year." It is one of the highest honors a children's book illustrator can receive. Brian Selznick won the Caldecott Medal in 2008 for *The Invention of Hugo Cabret*. Here are some other Caldecott Medal winners you may want to check out:

This Is Not My Hat by Jon Klassen

A Ball for Daisy by Chris Raschka

A Sick Day for Amos McGee illustrated by Erin E. Stead, written by Philip C. Stead

The Lion & the Mouse by Jerry Pinkney

The House in the Night illustrated by Beth Krommes, written by Susan Marie Swanson

and visit places they may not be able to in real life. "They allow us to imagine other worlds, to conjure events that we may not have experienced ourselves," he says. "That sounds pretty magical to me!"

Brian had a regular customer at Eeyore's named Laura Geringer.

He showed her *The Houdini Box* when it came out, and she said, "This is really nice. I'm an editor and I'd like to work with you." Brian was surprised. He'd known Laura for about a year, but he had no idea she was an editor. She wanted him to do the illustrations for a story by Pam Conrad called *Doll Face Has a Party*. Brian remembers the book as "this really weird story about this doll who throws herself a party and goes off looking for music and dancing and sweetcakes for the event. I was just so excited to work with Pam Conrad." Brian loved selling Pam's books at Eeyore's, and he loved working on her book. "When I finally met Pam she told me

Levittown, New York—
the setting of *Our
House*—in the 1950s.

that she had originally thought of the books as this quiet little story," he remembers. "She had these little Japanese dolls when she was a girl and she was picturing Doll Face as this very quiet little doll. She said, 'Brian, you've made it Broadway!' But she loved it."

In 1995, an assistant editor at Scholastic named Tracy Mack was looking for an illustrator for another book by Pam Conrad called *Our House: The Stories of Levittown*. Tracy loved the drawings in *The Houdini Box*, and she suggested that Brian work on *Our House*. She was thrilled when her boss agreed to hire him. Brian was excited too. He'd already worked with Pam before, and he had recently quit his job at Eeyore's to work as a freelance illustrator. So it was nice to have a new project.

"Browsing through the *Our House* file recently, I was appalled to discover that I had written a detailed illustration list for Brian, suggesting exactly what he should draw," Tracy says. This was a bold move for a young editor dealing with a brilliant artist like Brian. But Brian didn't mind the guidance at all. "In fact, he dove in with fervor," Tracy remembers. "He made a trip to Levittown, toured the town and surrounding areas with Pam, met with the local librarian, dug around in the library's archives, took tons of photos, read tons of books, and followed his immense curiosity wherever it led him. He

then created fourteen beautiful little pen-and-ink drawings, each one filled with detail and feeling." Brian brings the same level of enthusiasm and devotion to all of the projects he takes on.

Unfortunately, Pam Conrad died a few months after *Our House* was published. Although Brian hadn't known her for long, he was very upset. When Brian learned that Levittown was having a parade to celebrate its fiftieth anniversary, he was excited by the opportunity to march in Pam's honor. Tracy remembers Brian's enthusiasm for the parade: "We'll have to dress up, Brian told me. Everyone will be in costume…We would dress as the first citizens of Levittown, from the 1940s." Brian knew a costume designer

Levittown, New York in 1957.

who helped with their outfits. "Like a child eagerly anticipating his first school play, he couldn't wait for the big day," Tracy says. "He'd even made a beautiful sign with the book jacket on one side and the words 'In memory of Pam Conrad, who loved Levittown' on the other." On the day of the parade, Tracy and Brian were the only people who had dressed up! Brian was undeterred, however, and he and Tracy proudly marched all day in their costumes.

Brian has since contributed distinctive drawings to many children's books, often working with the same authors on more than one occasion. Brian illustrated the books in the Doll People series by Ann M. Martin and Laura Godwin. *The Doll People*, *The Meanest Doll in the World*, and *The Runaway Dolls* explore the world of dolls that come alive when people aren't looking. He did the artwork for Andrew Clements's books *Frindle*, *The Landry News*, *The School Story*, and *Lunch Money*. And he worked with Pam Muñoz Ryan on her historical picture books *Amelia and Eleanor Go for a Ride* (about Amelia Earhart and Eleanor Roosevelt's friendship) and *When Marian Sang: The True Recital of Marian Anderson*, as well as her novel *Riding Freedom*.

Brian's lifelong passion for dinosaurs shines through in his drawings for Barbara Kerley's *The Dinosaurs of Waterhouse Hawkins*. Brian says, "I've just been lucky that I've been offered these really great interesting stories with a lot of historical things I wouldn't have known, or stories I would never have heard. It's exciting to get a phone call from an editor who says, 'I've got this story I'd like you to look at.'"

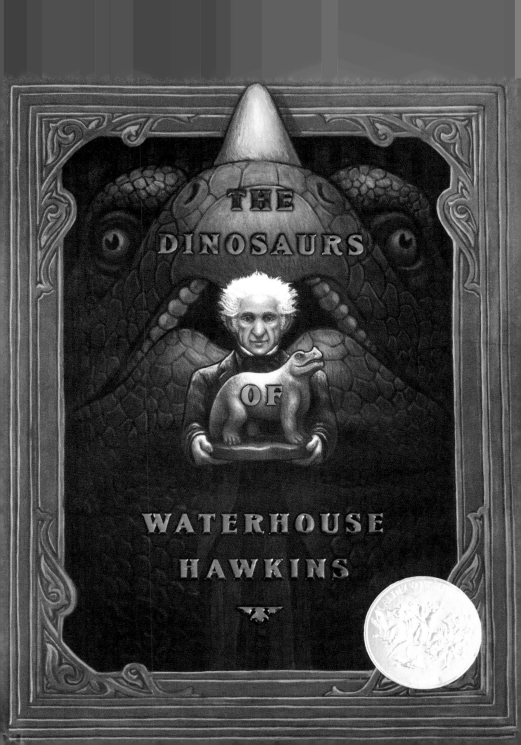

Brian's hero and
mentor, picture bo
author Maurice Sen

Chapter 3
HOW MAURICE SENDAK HELPED INVENT THE INVENTION OF HUGO CABRET

By 2003, Brian's career as an illustrator had taken off. He'd produced two more books of his own—*The Robot King* and *The Boy of a Thousand Faces*—and the illustration jobs kept rolling in. But Brian was dissatisfied with the work he was doing. He was mostly getting jobs illustrating biographies. A biography on the American poet Walt Whitman he'd recently illustrated was particularly hard for him. "Whitman just isn't a children's poet in any way," he says. Brian knew he didn't want to do any more biographies, but there was another problem: he had no idea what he wanted to do instead. Brian was depressed and didn't work for six months. "During this time, there was one thing that graced my life and saved me from going completely crazy," he explains. "I met Maurice Sendak."

Maurice's *Where the Wild Things Are* had been a major influence on Brian's work for a long time. "When I worked at Eeyore's, I finally spent time with it and completely fell in love with the book," Brian explains. "It's simply the best picture book ever made. If you want an education in the art of picture books, all you have to do is spend

A famous image from one of
the earliest sci-fi movies,
A Trip to the Moon

time with *Where the Wild Things Are*. It teaches you everything
you need to know." Of course, Brian and Maurice quickly became
friends. Maurice was reading Walt Whitman for the first time, and
Brian had just worked on a book about him. "We had these long,
amazing talks about Whitman's life and poems," Brian says.

Brian loved Maurice's books, but Maurice didn't know Brian's
work very well. "He asked me to send him a box of my books," Brian
says. Maurice was one of Brian's heroes, and Brian really wanted

him to like his books. Although Maurice thought Brian was a talented artist, he wasn't blown away by Brian's work. "He talked to me about my work, which he said showed great promise, but he steadfastly maintained that I hadn't come close to reaching my full potential yet," Brian explains. "These words resonated with me very strongly. I think I had secretly felt the same way. I talked to him about how lost I felt, about how I didn't know what I should do next. His words were simple but powerful: 'Make the book you want to make.'"

At first, Brian wasn't sure what to make of Maurice's comments, but he took them very seriously. "When someone like Maurice Sendak tells you that you have more potential than what you're reaching, you don't ignore that." Even though it was hard for him, Brian appreciated Maurice's honesty. Maurice's advice was good, but Brian still didn't know what book he wanted to make.

In the meantime, Brian read a bunch of books by other people. He was reading a book by Gaby Wood called *Edison's Eve* when an idea struck him. "I learned that Georges Méliès, the man who made the first science-fiction movie, *A Trip to the Moon*, in 1902, had owned a collection of automata, and at the end of his life they'd been destroyed and thrown away," Brian says. "As soon as I learned about Méliès's lost automata, I suddenly, mysteriously, imagined a boy climbing through the garbage and finding one of those broken machines. It was almost like a flash of light had gone off in my head. Here was the beginning of a story." The story became *The Invention of Hugo Cabret*—the book Brian really wanted to make.

Brian wrote an outline for the story and showed it to Tracy Mack. "Brian sent me the first, very preliminary draft of *Hugo Cabret* in the early summer of 2004. Though it was many transformations away from what it would eventually become, the kernel of genius was there from the first," she says. Brian spent the next two and a half years working on the book. "I got completely caught up in the story and the research," Brian says. The research involved watching lots of old French movies—like *Under the Roofs of Paris* and *The 400 Blows*—looking at real-life automata at the Franklin Institute in Philadelphia, and traveling to Paris multiple times. He learned all about Georges Méliès and watched all of his films. He even went to the apartment building the filmmaker once lived in and visited his grave. During this time, Brian met Remy Charlip. Remy happens to look just like Georges Méliès, and Brian used him as a model for Georges in the book.

The Invention of Hugo Cabret is over 500 pages long, including more than 300 pages of illustrations—but it didn't start out that way. In fact, it started out as a regular novel without any pictures at all. But Brian was influenced by all of the movies he was watching and wanted to tell the story like an old movie. "I started thinking about how you can turn the page and simulate some of the things that happen in the cinema," Brian explains, "the way that the camera can zoom in or pan across something, or cut from one moment to the next, or watch something unfold like a tracking shot." Brian started replacing words with pictures, and his 150-page novel quickly grew to 500 pages.

Nobody had ever made a book like *The Invention of Hugo Cabret* before. As Brian describes it, the book "is not exactly a novel, and it's not quite a picture book, and it's not really a graphic novel, or a flip book, or a movie, but a combination of all these things." Brian was a little worried that no one would read it. "I was working on a children's book about French silent movies," he says. "This was not a guaranteed bestseller at the time." Even Tracy Mack, who'd supported the project from the beginning, sometimes had her doubts. "What if we were way off the mark?" she wondered. "After

Asa Butterfield playing Hugo
Cabret in the movie *Hugo*

Martin Scorsese loved *The Invention of Hugo Cabret* and turned it into a major Hollywood movie.

all, a book that focuses largely on an old French cinematographer, early movie making, and mechanical windup toys is not really an obvious choice for today's young readers." Other people were more direct about their concerns: "While I was working on the book," Brian says, "there were people who said, 'You're doing a book about French silent movies and clocks for kids? That sounds like a very bad idea.'"

As it turned out, *The Invention of Hugo Cabret* was a smashing success! It was a *New York Times* bestseller, a National Book Award finalist, and a Caldecott Medal winner. Brian followed in Maurice's footsteps by winning the Caldecott Medal, which Maurice won in 1963 for *Where the Wild Things Are*. Maurice Sendak loved *The Invention of Hugo Cabret*: "He told me that this was the book he was waiting for, that he knew was in me," Brian says. "And that, of everything that's happened, is one of the most satisfying and amazing things."

Martin Scorsese also loved the book and made a 3-D movie based on it. Martin has been a filmmaker for a long time. He's directed some of the most famous movies ever made. And he knows a lot about movies. When he picked up *The Invention of Hugo Cabret* for the first time, he recognized the author's last name immediately. He hadn't heard of Brian Selznick, but he knew all about David O. Selznick. In fact, the first movie Martin ever saw was *Duel in the Sun,* which was produced and written by David. Martin liked the way the book involved the history of early cinema and the story about a son trying to reconnect to his lost father.

Brian visited the set of the film during production, which was a dream come true, and he even appeared in a scene. "It's such a thrill," Brian says. "I mean, Scorsese is the best, and when I went on set, everybody had a copy of the book. Scorsese always kept a few on hand, so he could give them to people so they'd understand what he wanted in the shot." Brian wrote a book about the making of the movie called *The Hugo Movie Companion*. "I love the movie," Brian says. "I think it's brilliant—and one of the most satisfying things to me is how faithful Scorsese and John Logan, the writer, and all the collaborators, were to my work."

Brian loved the combination of
words and pictures in *The Invention
of Hugo Cabret*. With his next book,
Wonderstruck, Brian takes that
format even further!

Chapter 3
WONDERSTRUCK? YES!

Working on *The Invention of Hugo Cabret* helped Brian develop a style of bookmaking that was unique. Brian was eager to use the format he invented again. "When it was time to do my next book," Brian explains, "I wanted to take what I'd learned and do something new. First, I got the idea to tell two separate stories, one with words and one with pictures, and then I started collecting ideas." One of the ideas Brian came up with was to tell a story from the perspective of a deaf person. "I had been thinking about deaf culture after seeing this really, really good documentary, *Through Deaf Eyes*, which is about the history of deaf culture," Brian explains. "There was a line about how the deaf are a 'people of the eye.' Most of the ways they communicate is visually. To me, that was the perfect reason to tell a story about a deaf person through illustrations." These ideas developed into Brian's most recent book, *Wonderstruck: A Novel in Pictures and Words*.

Wonderstruck alternates between the stories of two kids, Rose and Ben. Rose's story is set in the late 1920s and begins in

Hoboken, New Jersey. Ben's story is set 50 years later in the late 1970s and begins in Gunflint Lake, Minnesota. Rose is born deaf, and Ben loses his hearing in an accident. Both characters make their way to the American Museum of Natural History in New York City. Brian wanted his representations of deaf people in the book to be as accurate as possible, so he learned as much as he could about deaf culture. Brian was introduced to Carol Padden and Tom Humphries, two experts on deaf culture who work at the University of California in San Diego. "They were an incredible help for me while I was working on the book," Brian says. Brian also knew a deaf girl and interviewed her when he had the idea for the book. "I asked her if she dreams in sign language, and her parents said that they had never thought of asking her that before. She said that she does in fact dream in sign language," Brian explains. "I absolutely could not have done it without the talented people who are deaf, who helped me understand something that I just simply cannot imagine as someone who is not deaf."

In addition to learning about deaf culture, Brian spent a lot of time at the American Museum of Natural History. He knows a few people who work there, and they let him wander around the museum when it was closed. "In fact, the main genesis for this book started back in the early '90s, when a friend of mine...got a job at the Museum of Natural History painting dioramas and making displays. He invited me to come for a backstage tour. I remember walking around behind the scenes of the museum and seeing the workshops—a lot of the things that I actually describe in

The American Museum of Natural History is an important setting for Wonderstruck.

Wonderstruck—and thinking this would be a really amazing place to set a story one day."

Wonderstruck is a giant book. It's over 600-pages long, with one hundred more drawings than *The Invention of Hugo Cabret*. "I guess Wonderstruck does make Hugo look slimmer," Brian admits. "But I think the size may have maxed out with Wonderstruck. I actually do feel bad, especially about kids lugging these books around." Even though Brian had made a similar book before, the process of writing wasn't any easier for Brian with *Wonderstruck* than it was with *Hugo*. "I love writing and illustrating, but the writing still feels very much like a foreign language to me, because I'm thinking in pictures and I'm writing down the words," Brian explains. "It's sort of like I'm translating from pictures to words… So there's a lot more text description in *Wonderstruck* than there was in *Hugo*. And it's hard! It was really hard to write all of this description."

Brian attends the world premiere of *Hugo*, held at the Ziegfeld Theater in New York City.

Chapter 5
THE AMAZING BRIAN SELZNICK

Brian Selznick is amazing. He's made an outstanding career doing exactly what he always wanted to do: art. He's created the book he really wanted to make: *The Invention of Hugo Cabret*. And he's met and befriended two of his heroes: Remy Charlip and Maurice Sendak. His books have won tons of awards and *Hugo* was an award-winning movie. The success of *The Invention of Hugo Cabret* allowed Brian to buy a second apartment in the La Jolla neighborhood of San Diego, California, which he calls "Chez Hugo" (Hugo's place).

It's hard to imagine a more successful career as a children's book illustrator than Brian has had. But that doesn't mean things have gotten easier for him. Brian is an extraordinarily talented artist. He's also an extremely hard worker. And each new book is just as challenging as the last. "Every time I sit down to work on another book, I'm always right back at the bottom of another mountain, and even though I successfully scaled one previously, it doesn't mean I'm going to make it up the next one."

Brian's advice for kids who want to be illustrators: "I think the most important thing you can do is to keep drawing no matter what. And to not be afraid of drawing whatever interests you. If there is something that you want to draw, to make, then I think you should pursue it and not let anybody tell you that you can't do it."

PICTURE BOOKS BRIAN SELZNICK LIKES TO READ

Brian likes to read all kinds of books, but he mostly reads chapter books for older kids and picture books. "I love looking at picture books and seeing the beautiful drawings that other artists make and reading the stories," he says. Here's list of picture books he especially likes:

Fortunately, *Handtalk Birthday*, and *Thirteen* by Remy Charlip

The Leaf Men by William Joyce

The Borrowers by Mary Norton

Where the Wild Things Are by Maurice Sendak

Duffy and the Devil and *The Judge: An Untrue Tale* by Harve and Margot Zemach

It Could Always Be Worse: A Yiddish Folktale by Margot Zemach

SELECT HONORS AND AWARDS

Brian's books have received many awards and honors including:

Amelia and Eleanor Go for a Ride: ALA Notable Children's Book; Book Sense Book of the Year Finalist; *Parenting* magazine's "Reading Magic" Award winner

The Dinosaurs of Waterhouse Hawkins: Caldecott Honor Book (2002); Orbis Pictus Award Honor Book for outstanding non-fiction (2002)

Frindle: Christopher Award (1997); Rhode Island Children's Book Award (1998)

The Houdini Box: Texas Bluebonnet Award (1993); The Rhode Island Children's Book Award (1993)

The Invention of Hugo Cabret: 2008 Caldecott Medal; National Book Award Finalist; *New York Times* Best Illustrated Book of 2007; *Publishers Weekly* Best Book of 2007; 2007 Quill Award winner

The Landry News: Parents' Choice Award Silver Medal; SLJ Best Book of the Year; ABA Pick of the Lists

Riding Freedom: California Young Readers Medal (2000); *Parenting*
magazine's best books (1998)

Walt Whitman: Words for America: A *New York Times* Ten Best Illustrated
book (2004); Robert F. Sibert Honor for most distinguished informational
book for children (2004); ALA Notable Children's Book

When Marian Sang: Orbis Pictus Award for outstanding non-fiction (2003);
Norman A. Sugarman Award for outstanding picture book biography
(2004); Flora Stieglitz Straus Award given by Bank Street College (2002);
Robert F. Sibert Honor for most distinguished informational book for
children (2003)

BOOKS WRITTEN AND ILLUSTRATED BY BRIAN SELZNICK

Wonderstruck (Scholastic, 2011)

The Hugo Movie Companion: A Behind the Scenes Look at How a Beloved Book Became a Major Motion Picture (Scholastic, 2011)

The Invention of Hugo Cabret (Scholastic, 2007)

The Boy of a Thousand Faces (HarperCollins, 2001)

The Robot King (HarperCollins, 1995)

The Houdini Box (Simon and Schuster, 2001; originally published by Knopf, 1991)

BOOKS ILLUSTRATED BY BRIAN SELZNICK

The Runaway Dolls, written by Ann M. Martin and Laura Godwin
    (Hyperion, 2008)

Lunch Money, written by Andrew Clements (Simon & Schuster, 2007)

Marly's Ghost, written by David Levithan (Penguin, 2005)

The Dulcimer Boy, written by Tor Seidler (HarperCollins, 2004)

Walt Whitman: Words for America, written by Barbara Kerley
    (Scholastic, 2004)

The Meanest Doll in the World, written by Ann M. Martin and Laura Godwin
    (Hyperion, 2003)

The Doll People, written by Ann M. Martin and Laura Godwin (Hyperion, 2003)

When Marian Sang: The True Recital of Marian Anderson, written by Pam
    Muñoz Ryan (Scholastic, 2002)

Wingwalker, written by Rosemary Wells (Hyperion, 2002)

The Dinosaurs of Waterhouse Hawkins, Barbara Kerley (Scholastic, 2001)

The School Story, written by Andrew Clements (Simon & Schuster, 2001)

Barnyard Prayers, written by Laura Godwin (Hyperion, 2000)

Amelia and Eleanor Go for a Ride, written by Pam Muñoz Ryan (Scholastic, 1999)

The Landry News, written by Andrew Clements (Simon & Schuster, 1999)

Riding Freedom, written by Pam Muñoz Ryan (Scholastic, 1999)

The Boy Who Longed for a Lift, written by Norma Farber (HarperCollins, 1997)

Frindle, written by Andrew Clements (Simon & Schuster, 1996)

Our House: The Stories of Levittown, written by Pam Conrad (Scholastic, 1995)

Doll Face Has a Party, written by Pam Conrad (HarperCollins, 1994)

GLOSSARY

accountant—a person who manages people's money

archaeologist—a person who studies ancient human cultures by looking at things they've left behind like buildings, objects, and fossils

automata—a self-operating machine

Caldecott Medal—annual award given for "the most distinguished American picture book for children"

editor—a person who helps authors prepare their works for publication

illustrator—a person who creates pictures to go along with words in a book, magazine, or advertisement

CHRONOLOGY

July 14, 1966: Brian Selznick is born in East Brunswick, New Jersey.

1988: Graduates from the Rhode Island School of Design.

1989–c. 1992: Works as a bookseller and window painter at Eeyore's Books for Children in New York City.

1991: Publishes his first book, *The Houdini Box*.

1995: Meets Tracy Mack, editor at Scholastic.

2002: *The Dinosaurs of Waterhouse Hawkins* is named a Caldecott Honor Book.

2004: Meets illustrator legend Maurice Sendak.

2007: Publishes *The Invention of Hugo Cabret*.

2008: Wins the Caldecott Medal for *The Invention of Hugo Cabret*.

2011: *Hugo* (the movie adaptation of *The Invention of Hugo Cabret*) is released to wide critical acclaim.

2012: Publishes *Wonderstruck*.

Books

Do you want to learn more about the history and process of making picture books? There are a whole lot of books on these subjects. Here are a few good ones to get you started:

Marcus, Leonard S. *A Caldecott Celebration: Seven Artists and their Paths to the Caldecott Medal.* London, UK: Walker Childrens, 2008.

Marcus, Leonard S. *Show Me a Story!: Why Picture Books Matter: Conversations with 21 of the World's Most Celebrated Illustrators.* Somerville, MA: Candlewick, 2012.

Reading is Fundamental. *The Art of Reading: Forty Illustrators Celebrate RIF's 40th Anniversary.* New York: Dutton Juvenile, 2005.

Websites

Brian's websites include a short biography, a list of all Brian's books, links to websites he likes, interviews, information about Remy Charlip and Georges Méliès, a collection of essays, and a bunch of other fun stuff to explore. Check them out!

www.theinventionofhugocabret.com

www.wonderstruckthebook.com

BIBLIOGRAPHY

A note to report writers

Writing a book like this requires a lot of research. Thankfully, there's a bunch of information about Brian Selznick, including book reviews and interviews, on the web, in newspapers, and in magazines. Then, of course, there are Brian's books, which are the most important sources of all. All of the quotations in this book are taken from the sources listed here.

PRINT ARTICLES

Brown, Jennifer M. "Hugo Cabret, From Page to Screen." *Children & Libraries: The Journal of the Association for Library Service to Children* 11, no. 1 (2013): 35–38.

Mack, Tracy. "A Trip to the Moon, or, What It Was Like to Edit Brian Selznick's The Invention of Hugo Cabret, Winner of the 2008 Randolph Caldecott Medal." *Journal of Children's Literature* 36, no. 2 (2010): 67–69.

Mack, Tracy. "The Amazing Brian Selznick: A Profile in Three Acts." *Horn Book Magazine* 84, no. 4 (2008): 407–411.

Maughan, Shannon. "The Call That Changes Everything—or Not." *Publishers Weekly* 260, no. 2 (2013): 16–19.

Selznick, Brian. "Brian Selznick." *Horn Book Magazine* 86, no.4 (2010): 85.

Selznick, Brian. "Caldecott Medal Acceptance Speech: Make the Book You Want to Make." *Children & Libraries: The Journal of the Association for Library Service to Children* 6, no. 2 (2008): 10–12.

Selznick, Brian. "The Invention of The Invention of Hugo Cabret." *Journal of Children's Literature* 34, no. 1 (2008): 58–61.

Setterington, Ken. "Wonder Boy." *School Library Journal* 57, no. 8 (2011): 20–24.

Trierweiler Hudson, Hannah. "Talking With Brian Selznick." *Scholastic Instructor* 121, no. 2 (2011): 55–57.

ONLINE SOURCES

"Artist Profile: Brian Sleznick," The National Center for Children's Illustrated Literature, nccil.org/experience/artists/Selznick/

Brian Selznick, interview by Gavin J. Grant, IndieBound, www.indiebound.org/author-interviews/selznick

Brian Selznick, "The Invention of Hugo Cabret," www.theinventionofhugocabret.com/index.htm

"Brian Selznick Interview Transcript," interview by Scholastic students, Scholastic,www.scholastic.com/teachers/article/brian-selznick-interview-transcript

"A Conversation with Brian Selznick," Chicago Children's Theatre, chicagochildrenstheatre.org/see-a-show/on-stage/brian-selznick/

Joe Fassler, "For 'Hugo' Author Brian Selznick, Life (Thankfully) Imitates Art," *The Atlantic*, February 7, 2012, www.theatlantic.com/entertainment/archive/2012/02/for-hugo-author-brian-selznick-life-thankfully-imitates-art/252710/

Adam Gopnik, "A Deaf Boy's New York Quest," review of Wonderstruck by Brian Selznick, *New York Times*, September 16, 2011, Sunday Book Review, www.nytimes.com/2011/09/18/books/review/wonderstruck-written-and-illustrated-by-brian-selznick-book-review.html?pagewanted=all

Ed Vullimay, "Brian Selznick: How Scorsese's *Hugo* Drew Inspiration from His Magical Book," February 11, 2012, www.theguardian.com/books/2012/feb/11/brian-selznick-hugo-martin-scorsese

Motoko Rich, "Reads Like a Book, Looks Like a Film," *New York Times*, January 26, 2008, www.nytimes.com/2008/01/26/books/26selznick.html?ref=arts&_r=2&

INDEX

ABOUT THE AUTHOR:

Joseph Kampff is a lifelong student of literature. He loves reading Brian Selznick's books and he hopes you'll love them, too. He lives in Brooklyn, New York, with his wonderful family and their dog, Sadie-Belle.